BFI FILM CLASSICS

Edward Buscombe
SERIES EDITOR

Colin MacCabe and David Meeker
SERIES CONSULTANTS

Cinema is a fragile medium. Many of the great classic films of the past now exist, if at all, in damaged or incomplete prints. Concerned about the deterioration in the physical state of our film heritage, the National Film and Television Archive, a Division of the British Film Institute, has compiled a list of 360 key films in the history of the cinema. The long-term goal of the Archive is to build a collection of perfect show-prints of these films, which will then be screened regularly at the Museum of the Moving Image in London in a year-round repertory.

BFI Film Classics is a series of books commissioned to stand alongside these titles. Authors, including film critics and scholars, film-makers, novelists, historians and those distinguished in the arts, have been invited to write on a film of their choice, drawn from the Archive's list. Each volume presents the author's own insights into the chosen film, together with a brief production history and a detailed filmography, notes and bibliography. The numerous illustrations have been specially made from the Archive's own prints.

With new titles published each year, the BFI Film Classics series will rapidly grow into an authoritative and highly readable guide to the great films of the world cinema.

Could scarcely be improved upon ... informative, intelligent, jargon-free companions.
The Observer

Cannily but elegantly packaged BFI Classics will make for a neat addition to the most discerning shelves.
New Statesman & Society

CONTENTS

ACKNOWLEDGMENTS

For their help in different ways, thanks to Ed Buscombe, Sue Bobbermein, Tise Vahimagi, David Sharp at the BFI; the Japanese Cultural Information Centre at the Japanese Embassy in London; Brian Coe at MOMI, Robin Holloway of Connoisseur Video, Robert Whitehouse of Kodansha Europe; and Satako Nagai, Tony Rayns, Felicity Sparrow and Steve Beresford.

Act: To put in motion. To carry out an action. To carry out in mimic action. To perform on the stage. To perform on the stage of existence.

Actor: He who conducts an action. A stage-player.

Action: The exertion of influence. The thing represented as done in a drama. Gesture and attitude. Trained movements of the body. Active operation against an enemy.

Revenge: To extract retribution for a harm done to oneself or another. To punish.

BRISTOL 1967
. . . .

I was working in a theatre. In the daytime I helped with front of house odd jobs and in the evening I served behind the bar. This meant that I didn't often get to see the plays, though I wasn't missing much, just the same old English theatre of words. However, I did enjoy sitting in the empty auditorium during my lunch break, looking at the unpopulated stage sets and imagining what might occur. The dullest domestic sitcom interior, with backlit French windows, could become the setting for surreal scenarios in my imagination.

I mentioned this pastime to an intriguing man who came into the bar one night in dark glasses beneath a shaven head, atop a black, floor-length cloak fastened with a tasselled rope. He introduced himself as Dom Sylvester Houédard, a Benedictine monk from nearby Prinknash Abbey, and enquired what might be onstage at the moment. I said I didn't know, possibly very little because it was the time between productions, but when the bar closed I unlocked the theatre, switched on the lights and wound back the curtain to reveal the proscenium stage completely empty except for a large stepladder, the shadow of which was cast onto the white backdrop. Houédard sat in the front row and talked uninterruptedly for the next twenty minutes about the stage he gazed at, throwing in biblical, Tantric, scientific and Buddhist references to perception, whiteness and the void. Fascinated though I was by stage tableaux, I was nevertheless deeply impressed, and said so. 'Yes, yes,' he replied. 'But think how much more interesting it would be without that set of steps.'

Well, you might say that Dom Sylvester's viewpoint erred on the minimal side, but the more I did think about it the more I was convinced that there had to be a different kind of theatre from that of lines, prompts and glued-on side-whiskers. Instead a theatre of visual spectacle, spatial articulation, disorienting sound, music, colour and lighting, a theatre not of realism but of illusion.

I had always been drawn to such illusion. As a boy I had been taught conjuring by my Uncle Tom, a semi-professional magician who sold insurance during the daytime. In the evenings I would visit Uncle Tom, and in surroundings of stifling domesticity (the standard lamp in the corner of the living room, covers on the arms and back of the three-piece suite to stop it getting dirty) he would fan cards, multiply billiard balls, or pluck cigarettes out of the air. I gave my first performance of conjuring at the age of eleven as part of a variety concert at a mental hospital, changing water into wine in front of the rows of faces staring dumbly from behind the footlights and the uniformed nurses standing in the aisles.

At Art College in the early 1960s I did paintings, drawings and lithographs of stylised figures in theatrical interiors or artificial landscapes, influenced by variety shows, marionette theatre, the Commedia del Arte, ice-panto, Punch and Judy, opera and ballet. I also staged a ventriloquist act with a fellow student as a live dummy who sat on my knee. I was never quite sure what he was going to say. It was meant to be funny, but also slightly disturbing: who was venting whom?

So it now seemed appropriate to be working in a theatre, with an empty props room upstairs in which I could paint. But I wanted to get on that stage, and the opportunity arose when a cinema screen was installed and the building doubled as a BFI Regional Film Theatre, showing films in alternate seasons to the repertory of plays. In the change-over periods between the films and the plays, I organised, with like-minded artists from around the country, theatrical presentations which featured live action, film and slide projection, improvised music, taped sound and a variety of special effects. Now it would be called 'multi-media' or 'performance art'. But there weren't such categories back then; we were making it up as we went along, sometimes with unforeseen results, as when one artist, whose chosen medium was explosives, blew a hole through the pristine new cinema screen.

Subsequently the screen was invisibly mended, but I remembered where the hole had been and found my eyes drawn towards the spot when I watched the myriad of foreign films which now began to be shown. French, Swedish, German and Italian films, each one an eye-opener to someone who had grown up with the standardised diets of Hollywood and Rank at the corner picture house. Now I saw films *by* Bergman, *by* Fellini, and realised that films too could be personal creative statements. Film-makers made films, just as authors wrote novels and artists painted pictures.

Then one night along came *An Actor's Revenge* and the doors of perception were flung open wide. Here was that theatre of gesture, tableaux, illusion, colour, light, music and sound which I had yearned for. And all transformed by a visual artist into a CinemaScopic canvas as traditional and subtle as a Japanese scroll, yet as contemporary as the wide, saturated abstractions of New York loft painters and the Technicolor dazzle of Pop Art. When the unlikely hero, the Kabuki[1] female impersonator Yukinojo, having exacted his terrible revenge, finally disappeared beyond the horizon in a field of waving fronds, it was through the invisible hole I alone knew was in the screen.

The screen went black, the theatre curtains closed, and I sat transfixed in my seat, which I realised was the one I had sat in next to Houédard. The signs and portents all conspired to tell me: 'This film was made for you.'

LONDON 1994

Nearly thirty years on, I'm sitting in a cinema waiting to see *An Actor's Revenge* again. Many of the personal obsessions which caused me to identify so strongly with the film that first time have been developed in my own work as an artist during the intervening years, a selection from which has been touring the country, these past twelve months, in an exhibition called *Mask to Mask*: blank, impassive, imaginary portraits beneath which are other overpainted faces; audiences of painted, photographed and videotaped faces who appear to be in the darkened auditorium of a theatre, lit by reflected light from an unseen stage; mirror images of identical twins staring at each other from opposite walls. Speculations on role-playing, life as theatre, the society of spectacle, and what might lie hidden under surface appearance, not to explain it but to leave it ambiguous, while providing clues which stimulate the viewers' own imaginations, so that they in turn can speculate on what lies behind the mask according to their own mood and feelings which they bring to the pictures.

If, as adults, we retained the uninhibited reactions of the child we would be a source of perpetual embarrassment, so we all wear masks and tacitly agree to abide by social conventions of behaviour. It is probably the only way for civilised society to function, but if the masks become permanently fixed, then suppressed emotions can breed frustration which may subsequently either explode or implode.

To say that everyone is wearing a mask, that no one knows what anyone is really thinking, is disturbing and might seem pessimistic in implying that there is no truth in the world. Yet it is simultaneously optimistic because it also suggests that there is a hidden core in everyone which can never be quite plucked out and, for instance, can enable political prisoners to resist brainwashing, or hostages to survive months in blindfolded darkness and still retain their sense of self.

Since Bristol, there have also been a lot of films under the bridge; I've even made some myself, and now I know that making films is linked to budgets, fund-raising, production schedules, insurance, cost-cutting and compromise. Those Bristol days of naïve, unprimed revelation are long gone. Then, I'd never heard of film critics; now, every film is surrounded by evaluation, both in advance and in retrospect. I'm aware that some critical reappraisal of this revival of *An*

Actor's Revenge has mocked it as an absurdly cobbled piece of studio-imposed hackwork.

I wonder: will it still be possible to see freshly through this mesh of hindsight of which I was so blithely unaware when the film first entranced me all those years ago?

The two Japanese cinemagoers in front of me sit up straight in their seats and begin to fan themselves as a luridly orange artificial sunrise lights up the screen. The soundtrack bursts through the speakers with a melodramatic flourish of Bernard Herrmann-like strings which segues into a mournful Japanese song about reality and illusion, intoned by a sexually ambiguous voice. On to the sunset is superimposed the Daiei production company logo, followed by the film's Japanese title, *Yukinojo Henge*, subtitled *An Actor's Revenge* (though literally it translates as *Yukinojo the Phantom*).

Daiei was one of the five major companies who dominated the postwar Japanese film market. Daiei's studio boss, Masaichi Nagata, often called Japan's equivalent of Louis B. Mayer, is reputed to have occasionally treated Ichikawa's quirky individuality with a heavy hand, to have been angered by his unconventional treatment of sporting heroics in *Tokyo Olympiad*, and even to have suspended him for refusing to make the blockbuster *The Great Wall of China*.

Daiei also specialised in regurgitated genre material, and this is what *An Actor's Revenge* is four times over. Originally a popular newspaper serial by Otokichi Mikami, it was first adapted into a three-part movie series between 1934 and 1936 by Teinosuke Kinugasa, best known in the West for his highly experimental silent film, *A Page of Madness*. Kinugasa's triptych starred Kazuo Hasegawa in the triple roles of the effeminate Kabuki drag actor Yukinojo, the dashingly virile master thief Yamitaro, and Yukinojo's mother. Hasegawa was revealed as an actor of remarkable range who went on to establish himself as a prolific movie star, while the film became one of Japan's biggest money-makers.

In 1952 Kinugasa's three-part serial was condensed into a single film, with voice-over narration to link the disconnected narrative that resulted from the drastic editing. Cut in their entirety were the love scenes between Yukinojo and Lady Namiji, the merchant's daughter whom Yukinojo seduces in order to aid his revenge against her father. Only one atmospheric meeting between Yukinojo and the ghost of his dead mother, with spiralling optical effects, gives any indication of Kinugasa's stature as a cinematic innovator. Otherwise Kinugasa's film is a dislocated succession of martial arts fights and Kabuki performances, interspersed with static dialogue. The serial origins are evident in a ludicrous, will-he-won't-he suspense scene in which Yukinojo, attending Lady Namiji's funeral, is ushered into a room by her father, Lord Dobé, who attempts to crush him by lowering a false ceiling, but inadvertently brings it down on himself as Yukinojo escapes by the skin of his teeth. The whole dog's dinner is only held together by the skilled triple performance of Hasegawa. Nevertheless the truncated version continued to make money and does so to this day as a video release.

Even so, in 1962 it was still a curious choice for a remake by Daiei as a celebration of Hasegawa's 300th screen appearance, with the now pudgy and ageing actor reprising his twin roles as Yukinojo and Yamitaro. The Daiei management surrounded him with five of their most popular young stars in supporting parts, and they assigned the task of breathing life into the dated material to their top contract director, Ichikawa.

So yes, it was a jobbing commission, hackwork, but so were Bach's cantatas and Goya's paintings of the Spanish Royal Family. The trick is to alchemise the material. Now let's see how.

. . . .

The screen goes black and traditional *hayashi*[2] accompaniment abrasively strummed on a *shamisen*[3] is mixed very loud on the soundtrack. It sets my teeth on edge, like a knife down a blackboard.

A spyhole in the blackness opens like the shutter of a camera to reveal a Kabuki stage in a two-dimensional letterbox strip across the width of the CinemaScope screen. The back of a silhouetted head in close-up moves into shot on the extreme left of the screen at the same moment that the head in front of me shifts left to reveal on-screen a black and white circled parasol, like an eye which looks back at me through the letterbox slot. From behind the parasol appears Hasegawa in the role of Yukinojo the female impersonator. He is in white-face make-up and is dressed in a magnificent red and yellow kimono.[4] He twirls the parasol around the edges of the letterbox strip as he dances with extravagant, mincing gestures across the brightly lit stage, which is bare except for a stylised tree at the extreme right of the screen.

A cut alters our viewpoint to that of Yukinojos, out from the stage towards the audience. In a balcony box sits the beautiful young Lady Namiji, flanked by her father, the retired magistrate Lord Dobé, and the merchant Kawaguchiya. Namiji, seemingly hypnotised by Yukinojo's performance, parts her rosebud lips in a soundless sigh and places her left hand on her right breast as the eyes of her companions on either side look askance at her while still facing the stage. With a gesture mirroring Namiji's, Kawaguchiya covers his mouth with his right hand, through the fingers of which we glimpse a half smile. He is clandestinely watching her watching Yukinojo on stage, as we now do from over her right shoulder, as if we have joined the shadowy figures in the back of the theatre box.

Yukinojo continues his flouncing dance, his white clown face glancing up at the box as, in a voice-over interior monologue, he recognises Dobé and Kawaguchiya, who together with another merchant, the absent Hiromiya, conspired to ruin Yukinojo's parents and drive them to madness and suicide in Nagasaki twenty years earlier.

The faces of Namiji, Dobé and Kawaguchiya are each in turn vignetted in close-up, as if we were looking directly through the iris of Yukinojo's unblinking eye. Then the earlier shot of the group in the theatre box is repeated in a smaller vignette, reminiscent of a Japanese woodblock print insert or a strip-cartoon speech bubble, in the top right of the screen viewed over Yukinojo's right shoulder, as if we

Yukinojo dances in a midnight snowstorm during the Kabuki theatre prologue

were now viewing the scene from backstage; yet, as he sways to the right, the disorientation of viewpoint is further complicated by the group vignette remaining behind the back of his head before a jump cut brings us back to a frontal view of the stage.

Yukinojo whirls around the stage amid a blizzard of artificial snow, the vivid primary colours of his costume contrasted alternately with changing backdrops of blinding white and pitch black. Suddenly he stops and stands with winsome eyes cast down, swinging his kimono sleeves from side to side like a demure little girl as his tremulous interior monologue voice-over reveals to us, the cinema spectators of the filmed play, the terrible revenge he has decided to exact upon the guilty spectators in the theatre:

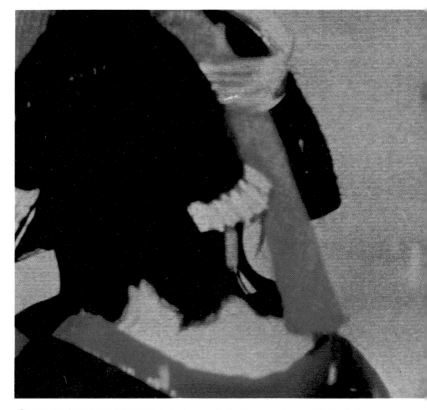

'Do you see them Father? They drove you to your death. Your enemies and Mother's. See how the girl is looking at me. I will approach her first.'

Do you see them, Father? They drove you to your death. Your enemies and Mother's. I have thought of them for twenty years. Now I see them for the first time. Now I shall always recognise those faces, even in darkness. No matter how difficult it may be I will avenge you both. See how the girl is looking at me. I will approach her first.

His mind made up, he speaks for the first time from the stage, a sing-song cry of 'Oh, you are there!', while pointing to the left-hand side of the screen, to which he staggers before collapsing into the cotton-wool snow.

From a stage-floor viewpoint the snow is golden in the glow of a

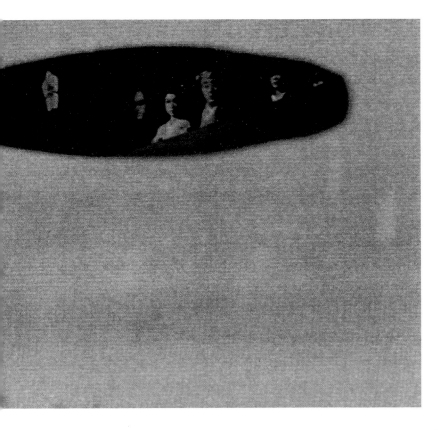

line of candle footlights, from behind which an old man holding a big straw hat above his head advances slowly from the darkened auditorium along the *hanamichi*[5] walkway extending from the stage. As he stands motionless over the prone body of Yukinojo, holding his hat aloft, the high-pitched, eerie sound of a *fue*[6] flute is cut short by a gong; he drops his hat, and strangulated yelling offstage cues *shamisen* and percussion which escalates in tempo and volume as the camera tracks back to reveal the audience in the theatre stalls, seen from behind and silhouetted against the golden curtain as it is drawn across the stage; they applaud enthusiastically, in unison with the two Japanese cinemagoers seated in front of me. The release of tension in both the theatre and the cinema is almost tangible. The breath I have been unconsciously holding exhales in a hiss through my teeth.

Thus ends the film's four-minute prologue, as perfectly self-contained as the famous opening sequence of another saga of revenge for childhood orphanage: *Once Upon a Time in the West*. But whereas Leone's preamble is then revealed to be a brilliantly deceptive red herring, Ichikawa's prologue, while playing games with the cinema audience's perceptions, nevertheless precisely introduces not only the plot and main characters but also the idiosyncratic visual and aural style he will employ during the next 109 minutes. So now, as I too applaud, safe in the knowledge that the film still retains its strange appeal after all this time, I can settle back to enjoy the labyrinthine unfolding of Yukinojo's revenge.

Wait, though; I'd forgotten that there is a second prologue which introduces the comic subplot featuring the exploits and jealousies of a group of petty thieves from the Edo[7] underworld who have also been watching Yukinojo's performance. The pretext for this subplot has as much to do with Daiei insuring themselves commercially by allocating cameo roles to a clutch of their hottest young box-office favourites as it does with following Kabuki tradition.

In the thieves' scenes which punctuate the film the humour is often leaden and the dialogue banal. Ichikawa amuses himself by juxtaposing their trivial chatter with ludicrously inappropriate background 'tension' music in the manner of Corman doing Poe, filled with strange scales, mysterious celeste chords and flute trills. The thieves, led by the feisty tomboy Ohatsu, act as a knockabout chorus who commentate on the development of Yukinojo's revenge. The master thief, Yamitaro, is good-humoured, virile but celibate, shinning walls like a human fly. Hasegawa plays the part of Yamitaro as well as that of Yukinojo, and it is this notable double performance which sustains the ambiguous relationship with the main plot.

The first meeting with his doppelgänger comes when Yukinojo, who in the tradition of Kabuki *onnagata*,[8] retains his feminine costume and persona offstage, is set upon at night, first by jealous samurai.[9] Yukinojo, in full drag, reveals himself to be an expert swordsman and sees off both the samurai and a band of villains with the help of Yamitaro. In the process they save each other's lives and are henceforth bonded like brother and sister. Their dialogue, with Hasegawa playing both parts onscreen at the same time, is the clearest example so far of the mirror imagery which abounds throughout the film.

The fight scene also provides Ichikawa with the excuse to indulge in a bravura display of visual and aural cinematic effects. In pitch blackness, faces are picked out in the reflected light from lanterns and flashing swordblades. A rope snakes across the darkness as the camera pans left, creating the impression that the screen has limitless width; then the rope resonates tautly in exaggerated perspective back into the inky night, implying that the screen has unfathomable depth. Sound effects of startling clarity whoosh, swish, clang and crack, juxtaposed with an utterly incongruous music score of cocktail jazz saxophone in a haunting minor key. It is a breathtaking *tour de force* as Ichikawa pulls out every trick in the book to whip the inert genre material into life.

Then the darkness lifts to reveal a section of grey, repetitively latticed wall which stretches the entire width of the CinemaScope screen. A wall without beginning or end, a backdrop, as if the whole scene had been played out on a stage (as indeed, in the film studio, it had).

Meanwhile, in another part of town, in a room saturated with yellow light, the avaricious Lord Dobé gloats over a ruby the colour of blood. Sated, he fastidiously wraps the ruby in a cloth, which he then places within a small box, which in turn he puts inside a bigger box before locking it in a safe. It is an image of fetishistic avarice which also symbolises the layers of hidden motive upon which the film's plot is based.

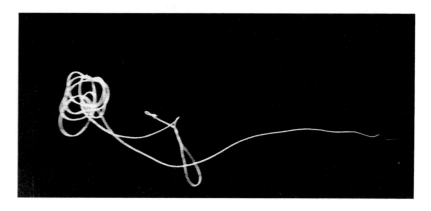

Curlicued arabesques become diagonals taut as bowstrings. The spatial articulation of a
canvas of infinite width and unfathomable depth.

Dobé arranges for Yukinojo to visit his daughter Namiji so that her love-sickness may be cured and he will thus curry favour for himself with the Shogun,[10] whose favourite she is. In other words, Dobé, behind his hypocritical fatherly concern, is pimping his daughter, his most precious jewel. His plan backfires, though, for Yukinojo's night-time visit only confirms Namiji's infatuation with him.

The love scenes between Yukinojo and Namiji are extraordinary. They kneel formally on either side of the screen in elaborate kimonos. Namiji, supported by an elbow rest, declares her love for Yukinojo while he flutters his eyelids and simpers coyly, whispering sweet nothings at the same time that his interior monologue, echoing the earlier one onstage, asks himself and us: 'How can I bear to tell such lies?'

Lush romantic strings play in the background but do not cue or react to the action or dialogue, creating the curious impression that though the couple are in a nineteenth-century traditional Japanese house, they could equally well be in a theme motel with piped-in Muzak.

Not a kiss is exchanged, not a centimetre of skin exposed except for faces and hands, as the camera pans around the silken furnishings of Namiji's peach-coloured boudoir, then slowly tracks along kimono folds and down the tresses of her waist-length hair. The contrast between visual sensuality and decorative formality, added to the sexual ambiguity of Yukinojo's transvestite role, creates an insidious erotic frisson. When their fingertips finally touch it is like a transferred electric current.

The double irony is that Yukinojo's deceitful seduction is tempered by tremulous eye and lip movements when his face is averted, which suggest that he feels at least pity, possibly even affection, for this innocent pawn in his game.

Yukinojo is also beset by periodic self-doubt about his ability to inflict the full revenge on his enemies:

> I am in torment when I visit Dobé's house. The wine I drink seems like molten lead to me. Must my revenge be like this?

Each time he wavers he reminds himself of their ruination of his parents and his resolve returns:

'Dreams are superficial. I know there is a daytime love deeper than the love of night.'

'You will be the only woman in my life.'

'How can I bear to tell such lies?'

They should be roasted. Boiled in oil. My parents will not be avenged unless these men are tortured until they become mad.

Rather than kill them by his own hand he utilises the full range of his acting technique, often in an unnervingly flirtatious manner, to exploit the three merchants' vanity, greed and jealousy, so that they will ruin themselves and bring about each other's deaths.

At this point Ichikawa steps outside the main narrative to toss in a disquisition, complete with roller captions, on the rice riots of 1836, ostensibly to explain the manipulation of the commodity market which Yukinojo will subsequently trigger. This uncharacteristic gesture towards documentary accuracy is contradicted by Ichikawa's spectacularly sensuous indulgence in the painterly potential of the wide-screen format.

Like previous technical innovations such as sound and colour, CinemaScope was touted at the time of its invention as another step towards greater realism, giving the viewer the impression of 'being there'. Ichikawa transcends this by laying a conventional soundtrack of portentous studio orchestra and plodding tympani behind a rapid-cut montage of grasping hands, abstract patterns of cascading rice and grotesque close-ups of anamorphically distorted faces. It is a virtuoso demonstration of editing, as if Ichikawa is saying: 'You'd like a little historical realism on the side? No problem.' You could take every frame from this sequence, Scanachrome each one onto large canvases, and you would have a contemporary art exhibition fit for any museum in the world, spanning the complete range from expressionism to lyrical abstraction.

Yukinojo, playing the role of tell-tale with hearsay from the palace, plants in the mind of Hiromiya the idea of bringing his hoarded rice to Edo to force prices down and thus be acclaimed as a great public benefactor. Sensing that he is about to enter his web, Yukinojo casts a sidelong venomous glance at Hiromiya, who is not looking at him, then in the same swivelling head movement switches back into his gossipy, simpering mode before making eye contact. 'Surely you would lose a lot of money?' he asks, as though ingenuously. 'You wouldn't understand about such matters,' Hiromiya dismissively replies. Yukinojo bows his head deferentially as his interior monologue returns:

He rose easily to the bait. 'We are like one family,' he says. But in fact he plans to deceive them. He knows very well what Kawaguchiya is doing: hoarding rice too. Their only bond is mutual greed.

Some days later Yukinojo revisits Hiromiya, who thanks him for his rice advice, which he has put into effect. By unloading his surplus stocks cheaply he has stopped the riots. They are interrupted by the arrival of Kawaguchiya, whose rice business has been ruined by the undermining of the market. Kawaguchiya attacks Hiromiya, who hurls him downstairs. A magical shot from the bottom of the stairs holds on the apoplectic Hiromiya and the inscrutable Yukinojo at the top, looking down. The screen gradually darkens except for a pool of light isolating Yukinojo's little smile and almost imperceptible hand gesture which indicate that his revenge is gathering force. Hasegawa's ability to speak volumes with the tiniest inflection of body language is marvellous. It is such a rare and delicious treat to watch a visual actor.

Kawaguchiya drags himself from the house and sets fire to Hiromiya's grain store. Hiromiya captures him and leaves him bound hand and foot, in an empty room without food or water. Yukinojo visits him there, disguised as the ghost of his father, whom Kawaguchiya had once ruined. He torments the terrified Kawaguchiya into head-banging mania, goading him mercilessly:

Hiromiya has financially ruined his fellow merchant Kawaguchiya and flung him downstairs. Yukinojo watches his revenge gather force.

Kawaguchiya, driven mad, is strangled by Hiromiya,

watched from the shadows by Yukinojo disguised as his father,

in turn observed by Yamitaro who scales the outside of the house like a human fly.

Hang yourself and die! Hang yourself as I did! Become mad, as I did! A man like you should never have been born. You cannot escape falling into the bottomless pit!

Then Yukinojo steps back into the shadows and watches impassively as Hiromiya arrives and puts the gibbering wretch out of his misery by choking him to death.

The first act of the revenge is now completed and the second follows hard on its heels. Hiromiya, now a fugitive murderer, is refused help by Dobé, and in desperation attempts to abduct Namiji. She momentarily rouses herself from her hypnotised torpor and stabs

In self-defence Namiji stabs Hiromiya to death in the dry-ice fog

him to death in self-defence. He dies with an earsplitting, gargling scream, and the strangely distant score of held string harmonics, vibes, *hyoshigi*[11] woodblock, very high flute and meandering bass clarinet disappears, to be replaced by what sounds like a theatre storm-machine. In mid-shot the scene appears to be taking place on a stage as Hiromiya collapses and dies in a replication of Yukinojo's previous 'death' in the Kabuki performance which began the film. Namiji is left holding the dagger, around the handle of which her fingers have locked; she prises them off with knuckle-cracking deliberation as the knife percussively vibrates like a rattlesnake, an implausible sound effect which is nevertheless gruesomely convincing.

When Hiromiya had confronted Namiji, they exchanged two lines of dialogue which could serve as a motto for the film. Namiji asks, 'Who do you think I am?' To which Hiromiya replies, 'And who do *you* think you are?'

From this point on Namiji lapses into a catatonic state, an insensible bundle who is carried like a rag doll by a passing thief to the house of Yamitaro, who summons Yukinojo as she begins to fade fast. She has fallen into a trance-like delirium, repeatedly whispering Yukinojo's name. She dies holding Yukinojo's hand, and the haunting flute music segues to the most cloyingly banal Hollywood strings, which serenade Yukinojo's tearfully remorseful deathbed speech as he tenderly administers the last rites:

> Namiji, you were so completely innocent. Life was unkind to you. You were born to be betrayed. A victim of your father's greed. A victim of my own revenge. You have died without having known true love. Not truly loved by anyone. Lady Namiji, if there is a next world I will try to make good my false promises. My vow may yet come true and I will marry you. I will never leave you. I will always serve you. We will be together. Lady Namiji, please do not hate me. Please go in peace.

Even at this tragic moment he is watched by an embarrassed Yamitaro: we do not know if Yukinojo's tears are genuine or yet another performance. Throughout the film his every action is viewed by others;

3 2   Yukinojo administers the last rites to Namiji. . .

he is never 'offstage'. Even when he walks by the lake, alone with his thoughts, we see him through the interpretative eyes of Yamitaro.

Yukinojo is a paradoxical variant on the theme of the 'lone avenger' personified by his polar opposite the samurai warrior (or in modern cinema by Clint Eastwood or Charles Bronson). Yukinojo has the samurai's moral code: fearless, self-denying and ready to give his life for family honour as the male heir. To achieve his ends, however, he uses feminine, not macho, wiles.

Then, in a scene which has macabre echoes of Dobé's earlier boxing up of his ruby, the body of his 'dearest treasure', Namiji, is unceremoniously stuffed into an ornate lacquered box and dumped on the doorstep of her father as Yukinojo initiates the last phase of his revenge. Before Dobé's horrified eyes he enacts in shadow play the suicide of his mother, whom Dobé had seduced with false promises and then driven mad. Hasegawa uses a third voice, different from that which he employs for Yukinojo and Yamitaro in this hallucinatory scene. Reminiscent of hooded Bunraku[12] manipulators, the shadow on the wall behind Yukinojo acts out the throat-slitting with slightly different gestures which are fractionally ahead of Yukinojo's. Unhinged, Dobé swallows poison and the revenge is complete. As Dobé's death rattle fades away, Yukinojo's face fills the screen, seemingly younger and serenely beautiful.

All the more startling, then, the harsh slamming of woodblocks and abrupt jump-cut to Yukinojo once more back on the stage of the Kabuki theatre, his face a grotesque mask of white pancake make-up,

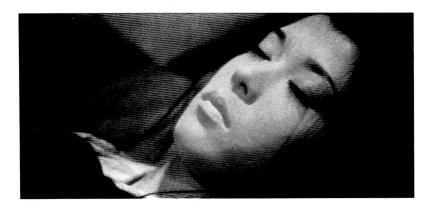

'Namiji, you were born to be betrayed. You have died without knowing true love.'   3 3

'Do you recall another face which resembled mine?'

'Thus my mother died.'

Dobé's poisoned death agony seen through the eyes of Yukinojo

in which his lips are a cruel gash of lipsticked crimson, his mascara-ringed eyes flashing like a tiger's beneath arched eyebrows. Powerful *shamisen, fue* and drums beat a strident tattoo, bit-part actors tumble at a flick of his fingers as Yukinojo stamps and shrieks in a triumphant dance which ends with him standing, arms aloft, at the top of a flight of steps as the curtain is drawn across the stage and wipes the performance from the screen.

Just as in the Kabuki theatre the final curtain does not necessarily mean the end of the performance but may, on occasion, precede the exit of the main actor along the *hanamichi* to the back of the auditorium, so there are three epilogue scenes which chronicle Yukinojo's exit from the film.

The revenge complete, Yukinojo triumphantly dances on the Kabuki stage during his final performance

'Many people sought him, the greatest of female impersonators. But no-one ever saw
Yukinojo again. Had he really disappeared beyond the windswept plain?'

First we see Yukinojo, in front of his dressing-room mirror, removing his make-up, the symbolic adornment which allows the actor to transform into a new self while still retaining the original self. Without make-up Yukinojo seems sad and vulnerable. He is watched by Kukinojo, the leader of the theatre troupe, who had vowed all those years ago in Nagasaki that his orphaned protégé would one day be avenged. Yukinojo confides to his Master that the harrowing experience of his revenge has forced his decision to retire from the theatre. We are left with the uneasy feeling that Yukinojo, who has pulled the vengeful strings with such devious skill throughout the film, has himself been to some degree acting under orders like a puppet.

The mood of pathos is broken by a cutaway to a seething *sake*[13] bar in which the characters of the comic subplot also recap on the revenge they have witnessed, but in a jocular manner. Duplicating Yukinojo's decision to retire from the stage, Yamitaro announces that he has decided to give up his life of thieving and go straight. Ohatsu snuggles up to the apprehensive Yamitaro, observing that in profile his face is rather like Yukinojo's.

To end, the huge persimmon, green and black Kabuki curtain once more fills the screen as the silhouetted audience leave the theatre. A slow mix through the curtain reveals the motionless standing figure of Yukinojo, in *onnagata* mode and dressed in a beautiful kimono, seen from the back in the middle of a field of waving grass. As the figure, which seems like an inanimate doll or puppet, fades into the distance in a series of dreamlike dissolves, a voice-over narration, by the veteran *benshi*[14] Musei Tokugawa, speculates on where Yukinojo disappeared to, never to be seen again after his final performance, and asks us to decide which of the characters in the film remembered the actor's revenge, as if the whole saga had been a second-hand story, or perhaps even an imagined fiction. And of course, as a film, it is both, as ambiguous as its hero, now completely vanished, leaving only the field of rhythmically waving fronds before a single woodblock bang cues a final black screen.

....

This final scene of *An Actor's Revenge* is like a parody of the traditional Western ending where the hero walks off into the sunset once justice has been done. Throughout the film one has the periodic impression that Ichikawa is directing this commissioned potboiler with tongue firmly in cheek, and having fun. He was never one to take himself too seriously – 'I don't have any unifying theme. I just make any picture I like, or any that the company tells me to do. There's a lot of Disney in me' – and this had led some critics to label him a mere cartoonist and illustrator, both of which epithets he accepts with equanimity, having indeed worked in those professions during his early career.

It's worth noting, however, that when Paul Hammond and I edited our anthology of cinemagoing, *Seeing in the Dark*, we discovered that first childhood experiences of cinema were most often of terror, and the film was invariably Disney. Ichikawa's immersion in Disneyworld is closer to that of the wide-eyed child than that of the sophisticated adult, tempered by his professional admiration for the way in which Disney, and his other great idol, Chaplin, both retained control of their work from creation through production and editing to eventual distribution, in a way comparable to a painter or novelist's autonomy.

Alongside Ichikawa's capriciousness and visual zest, there is another side to his character. At one time he divided his films into 'light' and 'dark'. The dark were 'not funny' while the light were 'more funny than not'. He placed *An Actor's Revenge* in the latter category, adding that 'if possible everything in my films has to be about something else'.

'I'm a very light person,' Ichikawa has said, 'so I'm irresistibly drawn to dark things.' Humour, bleakness, there's no contradiction, he argues. 'To me they seem perfectly complementary.' 'I look around for some kind of humanism, but I never seem to find it.' 'People want a happy ending, but doesn't the desire for a happy ending show how unhappy they really are?'

In interviews over the years Ichikawa hasn't helped his cause with purists by baldly stating some home truths which no self-conscious *auteur* would ever acknowledge. 'All of us who make films now have to compromise.' 'My own life experience was not very rich, so I decided to absorb other people's ideas in my own way, and see what sort of answers emerged from putting them on film.' How uncool, yet it applies to most film-makers, were they to admit it. Cheerfully to agree that you live by proxy is rather like filling in 'Fixer' on the profession section of your passport.

Ichikawa doesn't claim to be other than what he is: a contract film director who does his job as best he can. Often collaborating on the scripts with his wife Nato Wada, Ichikawa has consequently tackled a dizzy variety of subject matter: adaptations of serious novelists such as Yukio Mishima (*Conflagration*), comic strips (*Mister Pu*), harrowing war sagas (*The Burmese Harp*, *Fires on the Plain*), perverse sexual satires (*The Key*), grim psychological dramas (*The Heart*), sports documentaries (*Tokyo Olympiad*), and even a film seen through a cat's eyes (*I Am a Cat*).

A more accurate label for Ichikawa is his own succinct self-description: 'I was trained as a painter and I still think like one.' The visual and aural style of *An Actor's Revenge*, which strikes some people as artificial and baffling, is merely unusual because Ichikawa, unlike so many directors, sees film as an audiovisual medium, thus enabling him to treat a theatrical theme pictorially with a minimum of dialogue. He exploits the similarity of form between the Kabuki stage and the CinemaScope screen with a painter's eye, masking off areas of the screen and isolating images in the way that the Kabuki curtain is used to mask off sections of the stage and hide entrances and exits. The main Kabuki stage curtain is always drawn across, never lowered or raised, equivalent to a cinematic wipe or reveal. On rare occasions a drop curtain, revealing an unexpected new scene, is employed, with an effect similar to a jump-cut. Ichikawa parallels both effects, making cunning use of the sliding windows and doors of traditional Japanese houses to begin and end scenes.

An Actor's Revenge remains a benchmark of CinemaScope composition. It is one of those films, like Visconti's *The Leopard* and the Spaghetti Westerns of Leone, which are travestied by video release. To see them miniaturised and squeezed into a TV monitor is the equivalent of looking at a 35 mm transparency of a mural without a projector.

Sometimes Ichikawa saturates the screen with an intense yellow or blue, sometimes he sets off a spot of vivid colour against a white snowscape or dry-ice fog, or picks a dazzling highlight out of blackness. Just as traditional Japanese painters lovingly lacquered screens, so Ichikawa paints the cinema screen with a palette which uses the whole spectrum of hue and tone. *An Actor's Revenge* is the work of a visual artist composing for the stretched canvas screen with the playful dexterity of Matisse, Picabia or Hokusai.

There are interesting parallels between Ichikawa's struggle in *An Actor's Revenge* to make something lively out of the clapped-out format of the Kabuki movie, and the efforts of Suzuki Seijun, working at the same time over at the Nikkatsu studio, to reinvent the weary stereotypes of the *Yakuza* (gangster) genre, in films like the delirious *Tokyo Drifter*. Both directors used unrealistic theatrical effects, stylised colour co-ordination and saturation, eccentric framing and positioning of actors and props, spatial disorientations, incongruous use of music, narrative non sequiturs, sudden switches of mood, and an ironic portrayal of traditional Japanese moral codes, all wrapped up in a visual aesthetic of flamboyant style.

Suzuki was greatly influenced by the style of Kabuki, and in *An Actor's Revenge* Ichikawa also parallels his Pop Art collage of vision and sound with that of the most popular form of Japanese theatre.

Kabuki, from the verb *kabuku*, 'to tilt', signifies the deviant and unconventional. It never was a pure art form, but a magpie amalgam of stylistic borrowings. Evolving alongside the mass-produced woodblock print, Kabuki jettisoned the subtle hues of traditional Japanese art in favour of brilliant, garish colours. Ichikawa's visual treatment of *An Actor's Revenge* reflects this popular tradition, which extends right up to contemporary Japanese comics and video games.

Equally strident were the sounds of Kabuki, often referred to as 'aural colours'. The use of sound effects in *An Actor's Revenge* is exceptionally crisp, and the juxtapositon of music to visual image so bizarre that it jolts complacent viewing and keeps the cinemagoer in a state of head-scratching awareness. The surreal use of sound in the film reveals further kinship between Ichikawa and that other cinematic trickster, Sergio Leone, who was himself so influenced by samurai films.

What Leone couldn't have built a film around is Yukinojo. It is Ichikawa's masterstroke to reinstate the cross-gender eroticism which was edited out of Kinugasa's serial, and it is Hasegawa's magnificent performance in the *onnagata* role which lifts the film out of the comic strip and into the sublime. Hasegawa as Yukinojo is one of the cinema's greatest displays of acting. That it should be a cinema actor playing the part of a theatre actor makes it even more remarkable.

Theatre acting and cinema acting are two different things. I always thought that Laurence Olivier was a desperately bad film actor, the epitome of that thespianism which still bedevils British cinema. Whereas Robert Mitchum, even sleepwalking through the crummiest movie, was always a compelling screen presence. There is a quality of stillness which enables the great movie actors to command the screen without speaking a word. As Luis Buñuel used to say to actors: 'Don't perform.' Less is more.

Leaving aside the tremendous skill with which Hasegawa simultaneously portrays the physically opposite roles of Yamitaro and Yukinojo, it is his personification of the latter which strikes the perfect balance between theatre acting and film acting, criss-crossing the dividing line so subtly that the cinema viewer becomes unsure when to suspend disbelief.

The evolution of the transvestite actor in Japanese theatre is an important influence on the cross-gender complexities Ichikawa exploits in *An Actor's Revenge*. In the austere, aristocratic Noh[15] theatre all female parts were played by male actors, but formally behind a wooden mask, not employing the kind of female impersonation seen in Kabuki, and never using falsetto voices and mincing walks; whereas Kabuki was founded in the sixteenth century as a popular, risqué dance entertainment by the courtesan Okuni and her all-women troupe, many of whom assumed male roles. When the Shoguns clamped down on the brothels in 1629, they also banned women from the stage. Actors then took on female roles. They were known as *onnagata*: 'womanforms'.

Modern rationalists have argued that the female impersonator is an outmoded relic from the feudal past, and that women characters should now be played by actresses. Though vehemently rejected by Kabuki stage traditionalists, this notion has been accepted in Japanese films, allowing them to develop towards realism.

An Actor's Revenge is set in the period of the nineteenth century when the *onnagata* role had been developed into its most sophisticated and stylised form. Kazuo Hasegawa, before entering films, had been a leading Kabuki performer, specialising in the *nimaime* style of acting male parts, in which gentleness, vulnerability and a willingness to fall in love were contrasted with the *tateyuka* style, personified by the samurai who would sacrifice his wife and children out of loyalty to his lord. The *nimaime* style became particularly popular with women audiences. It is Hasegawa's unusual combination of elements from both *nimaime* and *tateyuka* within the third form of the *onnagata* that makes Yukinojo such a fascinating character to both men and women.

The ambiguity about the degree to which Yukinojo is 'acting' gives his character further resonance. He is acting a part in the theatre and retains the female costume and mannerisms of that role in real life. This notion is, on the one hand, absurd: imagine, instead of Yukinojo, Dame Edna Everage advising merchant bankers on financial manipulation of the country's staple food market, and those captains of commerce not only taking such advice seriously but acting upon it.

On the other hand, Yukinojo's transition from stage to real life is so smooth and consistent that it seems, paradoxically, normal. A double deceit seems sincere and inspires trust. Just as the merchants suspend disbelief when they watch Yukinojo's formalised stage performance from their exclusive theatre box, so they do when receiving him in their soulless designer houses, which are like stylised stage sets. Within these arid surroundings Yukinojo's unthreatening balance of decorous etiquette and coy flirtatiousness wins their confidence. They confide, and are then inexorably drawn into Yukinojo's patiently woven spider's web.

Yukinojo's feminine wiles are never merely camp. His recurring interior monologues, which stress that he is acting a deceitful part, each time catch us, the cinemagoers who are confidants to his secret, by surprise. Yukinojo's acting is so believable that we, like the merchants, also suspend disbelief. We thus remind ourselves that the character of

Fired up by ogling her *onnagata* pin-up book. . .

Yukinojo is also being enacted by Hasegawa for us, the cinema audience.

Ironic distancing devices which remind us that we are watching a performance are sometimes used by great screen actors, especially when playing preposterous or monstrous ogres. The risks of such knowing distance are self-indulgent pastiche and self-parody, but on occasion the artifice can actually increase the memorability of a character so that it becomes larger than life. In order to achieve this, the supreme film actors will even walk the tightrope of deliberate ham acting: Brando as the mythic Godfather, his cheeks stuffed with cotton wool; Mitchum imitating Victorian melodrama and grand guignol to portray the terrifying hellfire preacher in *Night of the Hunter*; W. C. Fields, breezing through his films with barely concealed contempt for the medium in which he is working, ad-libbing scabrous asides out of the corner of his mouth, the Lord of Misrule incarnate.

As a counterbalance, the interior monologue usually fulfils the function of revealing to the cinema audience what the character is *really* thinking. This inner voice may be one of realism or of fantasy, even both in the unforgettable instance of Travis Bickle in *Taxi Driver*: we eavesdrop on his thoughts as he moves with simplistic logic to the practical realisation of his horrendous fantasy.

In *An Actor's Revenge* Yukinojo's interior monologue is meant to show what his true inner thoughts are behind his scheming mask. The tone is one of sincerity but the words stress the mutual awareness of

Ohatsu propositions Yukinojo in the artificial wood

performer and cinema audience, simultaneously distancing him and us, at the same time as seemingly taking us into his confidence. The language is all about viewing and observing, like stage-instruction marginalia: 'Do you see them?', 'See how the girl is looking at me?', 'How can I bear to tell such lies?'

Yukinojo's inner voice is that of a spectator commentating on his own performance. This commentary is added to by the film's subsidiary characters, particularly the thieves who dog Yukinojo's footsteps. They discuss and comment on the plot of his revenge as if it were a peripatetic play being enacted for their benefit. The minor thieves are merely spectators, but the female thief Ohatsu and the master thief Yamitaro become involved in the drama.

'That face, that strength. His eyes send shivers through me. . .
But who could love such a half-man, half-woman?'

Ohatsu, who supposedly hates men, becomes, to her own annoyance, infatuated with Yukinojo. She is fascinated by his contradictory mixture of effeteness and physical strength. Sensuously she rubs the bruise which Yukinojo imprinted on her arm when he caught her breaking into Namiji's house during one of their midnight trysts. Lying on her stomach on the floor, flipping through a 'pin-up' book of Kabuki *onnagata* stars, Ohatsu muses: 'That face, that strength, what a strange man. He really has upset me. But who could love such a half-man, half-woman. I hate him!' She rolls over, squealing and kicking her legs in frustration.

As Yamitaro is to Yukinojo, so Ohatsu is a counterbalance to Namiji, whom she resembles in age and physique but differs from utterly in personality. Ohatsu and Namiji are played by different actresses, Fujiko Yamamoto and Ayako Wakao respectively, but Ichikawa cannot resist planting further confusion in the cinema audience's mind by intercutting between the two in playful reference to the mirroring of Yukinojo and Yamitaro.

Namiji is so listless with love that she scarcely seems capable of taking a step outside the cloying cocoon of her scented boudoir. She is a hothouse flower, her Western equivalent the sickly, swooning woman beloved of Victorian Academy male painters.

Ohatsu is a nimble, vivaciously tough little cookie who accepts no nonsense from anyone and is accustomed to getting what she wants. In contrast to Namiji's passivity, Ohatsu takes matters into her own hands. She propositions Yukinojo in a park, demanding that he take her to the nearest hotel for sex, otherwise she will expose his revenge plot. Yukinojo spurns her advances, so after failing to shoot him she settles for viewing from behind a tree as Yukinojo is set upon by three passing samurai. 'This is more exciting than stage swordplay,' she comments gleefully as she watches Yukinojo and the samurai fight it out in the theatrically lit park filled with blatantly artificial trees. As she watches Yukinojo, both in turn are observed by Yamitaro from behind another tree. 'I enjoyed watching your love scene,' he tells her after Yukinojo has made his escape.

Yamitaro, too, is fascinated by Yukinojo's courageous pursuit of his revenge, which he decides to assist: 'An actor's revenge. Dramatic as a play.' Yamitaro is also not quite what he seems, and is acting a

'I somehow feel as though you are my brother.'...

4 6   Yukinojo and Yamitaro, both played by Kazuo Hasegawa, onscreen at the same time.

part. Acknowledged king of the Edo crime world, when spied on by the aspiring minor thieves he is revealed as a Robin Hood character who secretly leaves stolen money on poor people's doorsteps.

Ichikawa frequently makes play with confusing cross-cutting between Yamitaro and his 'twin' Yukinojo. This mirroring is neatly demonstrated in a sequence which ends with Yamitaro, screen left, looking down at the prone body of Namiji. A cut reveals Yukinojo, centre-screen, also looking down at the same spot on the floor, but in another house, as if he has been a telepathic spectator of the previous scene.

Yamitaro also comments on the mixed feelings and doubts which Yukinojo has about the revenge, as if he can hear the interior monologue which we, the cinema audience, assume is for our ears alone. Spying on Yukinojo's machinations through rooftop skylights, or through blinds while hanging from a window ledge outside, he says wryly, 'He seems to be more than an ordinary actor', but suspects that 'He's not happy in the role, poor man.' Which we take to refer to Yukinojo's concealed distaste for being the Angel of Death, but might equally apply to Hasegawa himself. It must be unique in cinema history for an actor to be persuaded to play the same two parts, as sensitive romantic lead and muscular action man, thirty years after he originally portrayed them. Especially as the women characters who throw themselves at his feet are not comparably aged but remain young and beautiful.

Paul Newman and Clint Eastwood remained cinema heart-throbs into their sixties, and Al Pacino looks set to do the same. Each has cleverly adapted his screen persona to reflect advancing age. An equivalent to the unlikeliness of Hasegawa's role in *An Actor's Revenge* would be if Newman had been persuaded, in *The Colour of Money*, to reprise the part of Fast Eddie Felson he first played in *The Hustler*. The premise is so far-fetched that, while all concur that Hasegawa is mesmeric as Yukinojo, some critics have stated bluntly that he is too far past his sell-by date for the athletic role of Yamitaro. I disagree.

The most obvious first impression after seeing both the Kinugasa and Ichikawa versions of *An Actor's Revenge* is how little Hasegawa has physically changed in the interim. He always was pudgy and epicene. The speeded-up fight sequences in Kinugasa's film look as if they are from a Mack Sennett one-reeler and give a false impression of furious action. In fact Hasegawa plays the Yamitaro character at the same ambling pace in both films. In Ichikawa's version he resembles a genial, burly wrestler who has recently retired after a long and successful ring career but still keeps in light training for exhibition bouts and retains his supple strength. As such he seems, to me, quite adequate for the part, which is after all only an ironically twinning counterfoil to Yukinojo.

Yukinojo is the role where, after a thirty-year gap, the odds have lengthened inestimably against us being convinced that nubile young women get the helpless hots for a character verging on Widow Twanky. It is a mark of Hasegawa's astonishing acting that he can persuade us to suspend disbelief, aided by Ichikawa's direction skills. For if Ichikawa gets as much fun as he can out of the cinematic prestidigitation required to whip the genre stodge into a colourful dessert, he doesn't mess about when it comes to Yukinojo. Ichikawa knows that in Hasegawa he has an actor of unparalleled artistry, and he builds the whole film around Hasegawa's portrayal of Yukinojo. He superbly frames, lights and composes the whole screen for him in scene after scene, dwelling whenever possible in close-up on Hasegawa's extraordinarily subtle facial expressiveness. Like Pabst with Louise Brooks, or Sternberg with Marlene Dietrich, Ichikawa milks every last drop from the magnetic aura of his star. The result is that haunting images of the mysterious figure of Yukinojo linger in the memory long after the film has ended.

There are moments in the film when Yukinojo's face is as impassive as a Noh mask into which one can read any interpretation. The white screen without the set of steps. Then, like a light breeze suddenly ruffling a calm sea, the merest flicker of the eyes animates the mask.

Noh theatre is the original minimal art, and it's hard to see how a film could be based on it except by the Andy Warhol method of loading up a fixed camera and leaving it to record in real time. By comparison Kabuki is flashy pantomime, full of brisk movement, stops, starts and changes of scenes naturally suited to cinema editing. In Kinugasa's original version of *An Actor's Revenge* there are lengthy Kabuki performance scenes which become tedious interludes. Whereas Ichikawa uses to telling dramatic effect just a few minutes of theatre performance at the beginning and end of his film, and in between concentrates entirely on Yukinojo's offstage performance. Because Yukinojo's acting skills are allied not to gaudy stage spectacle but to 'real' life and death, they transcend the sentimental pathos of the theatre and have a tragic resonance. Hackwork is transformed into art.

EPILOGUE
. . . .

For years I was plagued with boring dreams. I would spend my days painting, drawing, filming or making collages, shuffling visual imagery into surreal juxtapositions: professionally daydreaming. At night, my subconscious mind would compensate with dream imagery of mundane dullness. I would dream of shaving, having my breakfast, going to the newsagents to buy a paper. I felt cheated by this stultifying, nocturnal penny arcade. I even edited a book of other people's dreams so that I could vicariously share their kaleidoscope of fantasy.

The only relief from dreaming in advance the trivia of the morning routine was occasional dreams which recapped what I was doing in the evening immediately before going to bed, and sometimes the bathroom-sink realism was tempered by intangible undertones. Just such a dream occurred after I had seen again, after such a long time, *An Actor's Revenge*.

From the cinema I had caught the tube, my mind still teeming with images from the film. I was acutely aware of the minutiae of body language, facial expression and every nuance of gesture. In the double glazing of the tube train window I could see the duplicated reflection of my face and its mask.

From the underground I changed to catch a crowded bus. I sat upstairs at the rear. In front of me were the backs of passengers' heads in rows, and in the front window were the reflections of all our faces, like another audience looking back at us. I got off the bus at my local pub and went in for a nightcap.

Three nightcaps later I had drifted into reverie. It occurred to me that the interval of years between Hasegawa first playing the roles of Yamitaro and Yukinojo in Kinugasa's film before replaying them in Ichikawa's was the same as that of my seeing *An Actor's Revenge* for the first and second time. A collage movie of images from my life during that gap of almost thirty years spooled through my head like that of a drowning man. Anaesthetised nostalgia, tinged with sadness, complacently filled my brain.

Enough. Time to go. I drained my glass and nodded farewell to the man sitting opposite, who I realised had been watching me as I sat self-absorbed. Half an hour later I was asleep in bed, but in my dream still sitting at that corner table in the bar . . .

... As in a mirror I saw a man, same age give or take a year, with the same thin face but a deeper frown, the same black coat with a black scarf, the same bony hands with shorter fingernails, his hair parted on the opposite side but of equal length, his left hand lifting his glass as I put mine down with my right. And in his eyes, brown like mine, I could see that this man had crossed the bridge where the phantoms had come to meet him, face to face. And the face which had been in shadow tilted up towards the light until the nose was level with mine, the eyebrows lifted and the lips said: 'So this is our last round. Now what will we have?'

In the half-sleep of dawn the dream faded, and all I could see were the hypnotic eyes of Yukinojo looking back at me from inside my closed eyelids. And all I could hear were those words whispering in my ears:

Who do you think I am?
And who do *you* think you are?

NOTES

. . . .

1 Kabuki: phenomenally popular form of theatre featuring gorgeous costumes, music and dance, characterised by satirical knockabout, mistaken identity, outrageous posing and visual ostentation. Frequently suppressed by the Shoguns as licentious and subversive. In contrast to the high culture of Noh, Kabuki was ribald mass entertainment. In style, a Western equivalent is pantomime, with its cross-dressing, Dames and Principal Boys, and vocal audience response.

2 *Hayashi*: the musical accompaniment to Kabuki theatre performances. It is usually of two kinds: *debayashi*, which is performed by onstage musicians; and *kagebayashi*, which is performed offstage and out of sight. The latter, as featured in *An Actor's Revenge*, uses *shamisen* (see note 3), flutes and a wide range of percussion including drums, bells and gongs. The musical range matches that of the forces employed, from melodramatic cues and flourishes, through intensely emotional counterpoint to the stage action, to uncanny evocation of effects which are more often created visually in other forms of theatre: crashing waves, rain, and even, it is claimed by virtuosi of the large drum, the sound of falling snow.

In *An Actor's Revenge* Ichikawa adds to the traditional Kabuki sound palette with celeste, bamboo mouth-organ, cellos, piano, tenor saxophone, pizzicato walking bass, vibraphone, musical clock, bass clarinet, fiddles, harps, tightly-muted trumpets quoting from 'Parker's Mood', and a glutinous conglomeration of strings. Often he uses the music wilfully to contradict a visual scene, as when Yamitaro and Ohatsu converse on an old fishing boat in the middle of a moonlit river, accompanied by the definitively indoor, smoky sound of chic club jazz sax, blues piano and trumpet obbligato.

3 *Shamisen*: three-stringed instrument plucked with a large ivory plectrum. Its bending, quivering notes can portray a variety of emotional moods, akin to slide and bottleneck guitars or banjos in Western Blues and Country music.

4 Kimono: this traditional Japanese garment, often intricately decorated, flattens and hides female physical characteristics, focusing attention on the face and hands. As the male characters of the period in which *An Actor's Revenge* is set also wear varieties of robes there is less gender difference in clothing than in the West where, until recently, the man wore the trousers. So Yukinojo appears more 'normal' as a transvestite than the Western drag queen.

In Kabuki the kimono is used symbolically as a layering device, to signify a character or mood change. In full view of the audience, threads are pulled from the sleeves and skirts by stage assistants, so that the top and bottom halves of the kimono are removed at great speed to reveal, in the blink of an eye, a new kimono underneath. The effect is similar to a 'before your very eyes' trick by a Western stage magician.

5 *Hanamichi*: a wooden walkway running from rear left of the Kabuki auditorium to the stage, used to heighten dramatic effect by bringing the action into the midst of the audience. An actor making his exit along the *hanamichi* would eventually disappear through the small *agemaku* curtain at the back of the auditorium.

6 *Fue*: a bamboo flute which produces a haunting, unearthly sound.

7 Edo was renamed Tokyo when the Imperial court moved there from Kyoto in 1868. Kabuki theatre of the late Edo period, in which *An Actor's Revenge* is set, had become decadent, employing an ironic distance from a tired genre, which is in turn reflected by Ichikawa's parodic cinema treatment.

8 *Onnagata*: Kabuki female impersonators, admired equally by men and women audiences. One of the greatest was Yoshizawa Ayame (1653–1729), who initiated the custom of retaining female costume and mannerisms offstage in order to immerse oneself in the role. This rule of stagecraft is used to Machiavellian effect by Yukinojo in *An Actor's Revenge*.

9 Samurai: a warrior class retainer in the pay of the Shoguns and other regional lords. A conservative, socially elite hired sword. Often homosexual and definitively macho, the samurai favoured Noh theatre and were contemptuous of the effeminate campness of Kabuki.

10 Shogun: a feudal military potentate, often keeping a harem. Lady Namiji, euphemistically referred to in *An Actor's Revenge* as a 'favourite' of the Shogun, in fact has none of the characteristics of the Kabuki courtesan but all the precious lassitude of the Kabuki virgin princess.

11 *Hyoshigi*: a pair of clappers of hard wood, struck by a Kabuki stage assistant to mark the drawing of the curtain at the beginning or end of a scene, or at moments of dramatic climax. Striking starts some minutes before the final curtain is drawn, at first isolated clicks, then finally in a continuous clatter; this effect is used at the end of the Kabuki prologue in *An Actor's Revenge*.

12 Bunraku: traditional Japanese puppet theatre, many of whose plots were borrowed and adapted by the Kabuki theatre in the eighteenth century. In Bunraku the puppeteers manipulate the realistic rod puppets, which are over one metre high, in full view of the audience, but deflect the audience's attention away from their manipulations either by cloaking and hooding themselves in black or by making their own movements lifeless and their countenances impassive. Comparable diversionary tactics are used by Western ventriloquists. In *An Actor's Revenge* Yukinojo, seemingly passive and self-effacing, actually manipulates all those who are instrumental to his revenge.

Ichikawa's first film, *Girl at the Dojo Temple* (1946), was puppet animation based on a famous Kabuki dance. Because the script had not been submitted for approval the Occupation authorities seized the negative and it has never been found.

13 *Sake*: a colourless alcoholic beverage made from rice and served in small, heated flasks. Its deceptively bland taste, like warm scented bathwater, is belied by the failure of the inexperienced drinker's legs to function when attempting to rise from a sitting position after dinner.

14 *Benshi*: colloquially known as a 'movie talker', who in the early days of Japanese cinema would stand alongside the screen and interpret the onscreen action for the cinema audience. In *An Actor's Revenge* the use of *benshi* voice-over in the final scene adds one last commentary device which brings the film full circle from the opening credits song about 'reality' and 'illusion'.

15 *Noh*: the oldest, most austere and stately form of Japanese theatre, aspiring to induce in the spectator a state of dreamlike contemplation of the human predicament in its elemental form, during extremely slow performances lasting several hours.

CREDITS
. . . .
An Actor's Revenge (Yukinojo Henge)

Japan
1962
Production Company
Daiei Kyoto
Producer
Masaichi Nagata
Production Manager
Tadao Murakami
Planning
Kon Ichikawa
Komei Fujii
Tomio Takamori
Director
Kon Ichikawa
Assistant Directors
Akira Inoue
Masuya Nakamura
Screenplay
Natto Wada
Based on the *Asahi*
newspaper serial
by Otokichi Mikami
and the screenplay
by Daisuke Ito,
Teinosuke Kinugasa
Director of Photography
Setsuo Kobayashi
DaieiScope
Colour
Daiei-color
Lighting
Kenichi Okamoto
Colour Technician
Toshio Kajitani
Editor
Shigeo Nishida
Art Director
Yoshinobu Nishioka
Costume Adviser
Yoshio Ueno
Music
Japanese:
Tamekichi Mochizuki
Ancient:
Yahichi Takezawa
Additional:
Yasushi Akutagawa
Masao Yagi

Choreography
Action:
Shohei Miyauchi
Stage:
Kangoro Fujima
Collaborators
Kazuo Ikehiro
Senkichiro Takeda
Hiroyo Kato
Sound Recordist
Gen Otani
Sound Effects
Noburu Kurashima
10,170 feet
113 minutes

Kazuo Hasegawa
Yukinojo Nakamura/
Yamitaro the Thief
Fujiko Yamamoto
Ohatsu
Ayako Wakao
Namiji
Eiji Funakoshi
Heima Kadokura
Narutoshi Hayashi
Mukuzu, Ohatsu's
partner
Eijiro Yanagi
Hiromiya
Chusha Ichikawa
Kikunojo Nakamura
Ganjiro Nakamura
Sansai Dobé
Saburo Date
Kawaguchiya
Jun Hamamura
Isshosai
Kikue Mori
Cruel old woman
Masayoshi Kikuno
Yukinojo's father
Raizo Ichikawa
Hirutaro
Shintaro Katsu
Hojin, fugitive from
Prison Island

Yutaka Nakamura
Townsman
Chitose Maki
Townswoman
Toshiro Chiba
Ronin
Koichi Mizuhara
Dobé's man
Tadashi Kato
Shogun's retainer
Eigoro Onoe
Shogun
Shiro Otsuji
Tokio Oki
Civil Guardsmen
Musei Tokugawa
Narrator
Hajime Koshigawa
Akira Shiga
Gen Kimura
Takeo Inoue
Takeshi Yabuya
Jun Arimura
Akira Konami
Keiko Koyanagi

Credits checked by Markku
Salmi. The print of *An
Actor's Revenge* in the
National Film and
Television Archive was
specially acquired from the
National Film Centre,
Tokyo, with generous
assistance from Peter
Palumbo.
Available on VHS in the
UK on the Connoisseur
Video label.

BIBLIOGRAPHY

. . . .

1. Books

Audie Bock. *Japanese Film Directors* (Tokyo: Kodansha, 1978).

Ian Breakwell and Paul Hammond (eds.). *Seeing in the Dark* (London: Serpents Tail, 1990).

Simon Field and Tony Rayns (eds.). *Branded to Thrill: the delirious cinema of Suzuki Seijun* (London: ICA and Japan Foundation, 1994).

Masakatsu Gunji and Chiaki Yoshida. *The Kabuki Guide* (Tokyo: Kodansha, 1987).

Donald Keene. *Bunraku* (Tokyo: Kodansha, 1974).

Kunio Komparu. *The Noh Theatre* (New York/ Tokyo: Weatherill and Tankosha, 1983).

Matzo Nakamura. *Kabuki, Backstage, Onstage* (Tokyo: Kodansha, 1990).

Tadao Sato. *Currents in Japanese Cinema* (Tokyo: Kodansha, 1982).

2. Articles

Ian Breakwell. 'Mask to Mask', *AND* no. 28, 1993.

Brian Powell. 'Japanese Theatre', *Contemporary Theatre Review*, March 1994.

Donald Richie. 'The Several Sides of Kon Ichikawa', *Sight and Sound*, vol. 35 no. 2, pp. 84–6, 1966.

David Williams. 'An Actor's Revenge', *Screen*, March/April 1970.

3. Reviews

Tony Rayns. *Sight and Sound*, vol. 3 (NS) no. 5, (May 1993), pp. 61–2.

David Robinson. *Financial Times* (17 March 1967).

Richard Roud. *Guardian* (17 March 1967).

David Wilson. *Monthly Film Bulletin*, vol. 34, no. 400 (May 1967), pp. 73–4.

ALSO PUBLISHED

If you would like further Information about future BFI Film Classics or about other books on film, media and popular culture from BFI Publishing, please write to:

**BFI Film Classics
British Film Institute
21 Stephen Street
London
W1P 2LN**

**BFI Film Classics '... could scarcely be
improved upon ... informative, intelligent,
jargon-free companions.'**
The Observer

Each book in the BFI Publishing Film Classics series
honours a great film from the history of world cinema.
With new titles published each year, the series is rapidly
building into a collection representing some of the best
writing on film. If you would like to receive further
information about future Film Classics or about other
books from BFI Publishing, please fill in your name and
address and return this card to the BFI.*
No stamp is needed if posted in the UK, Channel
Islands, or Isle of Man.

NAME

ADDRESS

POSTCODE

*North America: Please return your card to:
Indiana University Press, Attn: LPB, 601 N Morton Street,
Bloomington, IN 47401-3797

**BFI Publishing
21 Stephen Street
FREEPOST 7
LONDON
W1E 4AN**